April's Bake Shop

by Lisa Boggs
illustrated by Yvette Banek

Core Decodable 61

Mc Graw Hill Education

Bothell, WA • Chicago, IL • Columbus, OH • New York, NY

MHEonline.com

Copyright © 2015 McGraw-Hill Education

All rights reserved. No part of this publication may be reproduced or distributed in any form or by any means, or stored in a database or retrieval system, without the prior written consent of McGraw-Hill Education, including, but not limited to, network storage or transmission, or broadcast for distance learning.

Send all inquiries to:
McGraw-Hill Education
8787 Orion Place
Columbus, OH 43240

ISBN: 978-0-02-145085-5
MHID: 0-02-145085-4

Printed in the United States of America.

2 3 4 5 6 7 8 9 DOC 20 19 18 17 16 15

Down the block is a shop.
It's April's Bake Shop.

April prints a paper label.
She marks "Bread for Sale."

There is her table.
There is her plate.
What happened to her bread?

Birds sit on top of her shop.
Birds ate her bread!